SLOW COOKER DUMP DINNERS

SLOW COOKER DUMP DINNERS

5-INGREDIENT RECIPES FOR MEALS THAT (PRACTICALLY) COOK THEMSELVES

JENNIFER PALMER

THE COUNTRYMAN PRESS · WOODSTOCK, VT.

The Countryman Press
www.countrymanpress.com

A division of W. W. Norton & Company, Inc.,
500 Fifth Avenue, New York, NY 10110
www.wwnorton.com

For information about special discounts for bulk purchases, please contact W. W. Norton Special Sales at specialsales@wwnorton.com or 800-233-4830.

Printed in the United States

Library of Congress Cataloging-in-Publication Data

Palmer, Jennifer, 1980–
Slow cooker dump dinners : 5-ingredient recipes for meals that (practically) cook themselves / Jennifer Palmer.
      pages cm
Includes index.
ISBN 978-1-58157-334-3 (pbk.)
1. Electric cooking, Slow. 2. Quick and easy cooking. I. Title.
TX827.P34 2015
641.5'884—dc23
                              2015018976

10 9 8 7 6 5 4

TO BUSY PEOPLE, EVERYWHERE

SLOW COOKER DUMP DINNERS
CONTENTS

INTRODUCTION / 9

Chapter One: Chicken / 15

Chicken Thighs with
Potatoes and Carrots

Spicy Chicken Avocado Soup

Buffalo Blue Cheese
Chicken Sliders

Chicken Noodle Soup

Shredded Barbeque Chicken

Orange Chicken Drumsticks

Herbed Roast Chicken

Italian Parmesan Chicken

Dad's Famous Chicken Curry

Salsa Verde Chicken

Sweet Potato and Kale
Chicken Stew

Chicken and Cashew Medley

Tuscan Chicken Alfredo

Chicken Tikka Masala

Drunken Cornish Hens

Slow Cooker Pot Pie

Chicken-Apple Sausage with
Sweet Potatoes

Chapter Two: Pork / 51

Kale, Sausage, and White
Bean Soup

Simple Sausage Jambalaya

Kielbasa and Carrot Medley

Rosemary Herbed Pork
Chops

Pulled Pork

Baby Back Ribs

Potato Bacon Casserole

Bacon Baked Beans

Breakfast-For-Dinner
Casserole

Chapter Three: Beef / 71

Broccoli Beef

Beef Brisket

Cowboy Beef Tacos

Corned Beef and Cabbage

Classic Chili

Cheesy Stuffed Peppers

Easy Beef Stroganoff

Classic Family-Style
Meat Loaf

Steak and Mushrooms
with Gravy

Hearty Shepherd's Pie

Italian Dip Sandwiches

Family-Style Pot Roast

BBQ Meatball Sandwiches

Southwest Meatball Stew

Quick and Easy Lasagna

Chapter Four: Fish and Seafood / 103

New England Clam Chowder

Hearty Shrimp Gumbo

Poached Salmon Fillets

Chapter Five: Vegetarian / 111

Tortellini Soup

Stuff-Your-Own
Baked Potatoes

Green Lentil Curry

Country-Style Macaroni
and Cheese

Black Bean and
Corn Enchiladas

Two Corn Chowder

ACKNOWLEDGMENTS / 125

INDEX / 126

Introduction: Welcome to Slow Cooker Dump Dinners!

It's no secret, slow cookers are the best! Who doesn't love dumping a bunch of ingredients into a pot before rushing off to work or to run errands—and coming home hours later to a perfectly cooked meal? That's the joy of Slow Cooker Dump Dinners. They're an essential option for any busy household. What makes this slow cooker book unusual is that all the recipes require just five ingredients or fewer, plus herbs and spices! Instead of recipes that require a grocery list that's ten items (or more) long, I've kept it simple (and less expensive). Included here are the best recipes I've tried and tested and I can't wait to share them with you.

Some Notes about the Recipes

5 Ingredients: The recipes all have five primary ingredients, plus spices, so don't worry if the list seems long.

Serving size: These recipes will generally feed two or three adults with leftovers or two adults and two children unless otherwise noted, but use your best judgment—if you have a hungry teenager at home you may want to double the recipe! These recipes can all be made in a 6-quart slow cooker although many can fit in a 4-quart size (that's what works best for me and my husband in our tiny New York kitchen).

Cooking from frozen: You can precook many of these recipes and cook them straight from the freezer (see the Freezer + Slow Cooker = Easiest Dinners Ever section). Most of the recipes here call for frozen vegetables. You can easily substitute the same amount of fresh vegetables if you prefer or if that's what you have on hand.

CHOOSING A SLOW COOKER

Slow cookers come in varying sizes with loads of different features, so it's important to determine your needs before you go shopping.

I've listed four most important considerations when choosing a slow cooker:

1. Size: The first consideration when selecting a slow cooker is probably the size. Slow cookers come in capacities ranging from 1.5 quarts to 12 quarts or larger. If you're cooking for yourself or one other person, the 1.5-quart or 4-quart is probably right for you. If you regularly cook for a large number of people or cook in large batches and freeze your recipes, an 8- or 12-quart may be what you're looking for.
2. Automation: Not all slow cookers are created equal. If you're looking for one with a programmable timer and automatic shut-off you'll have to pay a bit more. Slow cookers with a simple knob that turns to low, medium, or high are easy to use but require more attention, as you have to remember to shut them off.
3. Portability: Some slow cookers come with metal fasteners that fix the glass lid to the base of the slow cooker, which allows you to transport the appliance easily with no mess. If you're often off to potlucks or family dinners this may be worth investigating.
4. Multitasking: Some slow cookers come with two pots in one unit. This lets you cook two different recipes at the same time—so if you want soup as your starter and pork chops for your main course, a unit like this may be worth considering.

TIPS FOR HEALTHY SLOW COOKING

If eating healthier is your goal, there are a few easy adjustments to help make your slow cooker recipes even better for you and your family. Here are a few key things you can do to help you maintain your healthy objectives.

1. If you want to reduce your sodium intake: Use low-sodium or reduced-sodium broth and soy sauce for your recipes.
2. If you want to eat less red meat: When a recipe calls for ground beef, try swapping it out for lean ground turkey instead.
3. If you want to eat more vegetables: Add your favorite vegetables to any recipe. If you've mastered the bacon and potato casserole for example, try adding mushrooms or broccoli next time.
4. If you want to reduce your fat intake: Try using low-fat dairy products or slightly reducing the amount of butter or cheese in a recipe. Garnish with cilantro or spring onion rather than cheese or sour cream.

TIPS FOR USING YOUR SLOW COOKER

1. Slow cooker liners: Slow cookers keep your clean-up time to a minimum. But to make things even easier for you, some brands have developed single-use slow cooker liners that fit inside. Once you're done cooking, just throw the liner away with no additional washing required. You can achieve this same effect by creating a do-it-yourself aluminum foil liner as well.

2. Browning the meat: Some people swear by this method. If you find the texture of the meat in your recipes is just lacking a certain something, try quickly browning your steaks or chicken in a skillet with a bit of oil before adding them to the slow cooker.

3. Adding liquid: Some slow cookers may keep hotter than others, so to ensure your dinner is as juicy and tender as possible feel free to add in extra liquid at any stage. A half cup of hot water or broth should do the trick.

Remember, the point of a slow cooker is to make cooking as easy and as painless as possible! So have fun with the recipes and experiment as you go. Happy slow cooking!

FREEZER + SLOW COOKER = EASIEST DINNERS EVER

By planning ahead you can make your slow cooking experience even easier. How? By cooking and freezing the entire recipe (or just certain ingredients) ahead of time. Just remember these four easy steps:

1. Prepare the recipe and place into a freezer-safe container
2. Label it with the recipe name, cooking instructions, and the date
3. Freeze it
4. Slow cook it!

A good place to begin is to choose your five meals for the week, head to the grocery store to get the necessary ingredients, and take an afternoon to prepare all the meals. Once you see how easy it is to pull full meals from the freezer and dump them into your slow cooker you'll want to keep doing it. In general, things like chili, soups, and curries make great freezer meals.

In addition to full meals, it's also handy to prepare specific ingredients ahead of time. Things like pasta, rice, sautéed vegetables, or ground beef are great to have ready-made. Remember to freeze in family-sized portions (1 cup of cooked rice or pasta per person, for example). Anything that may require additional prep time before you can enjoy your meal—make it ahead of time and freeze it.

Notes on Frozen Dinner Preparation

Always thaw your frozen dinners before placing them in the slow cooker. This is to ensure the meat is thoroughly cooked before serving. Thaw the meals in the fridge—never leave them out at room temperature.

Once you've made your meals for the week, you can put the first two straight into the fridge. When you use a meal from the fridge, remember to replace it with one from the freezer so you always have a thawed meal on hand.

Vegetarian meals and ingredients can be cooked directly from frozen.

Avoid freezing potatoes whenever possible. They tend to get mushy when thawed.

Avoid freezing dairy products like cheese or cream cheese. They can separate, curdle, and lose texture. Eggs also should not be frozen.

Use freezer-safe containers or plastic freezer bags. Remember to label each container with the contents and the date on a freezer label or piece of tape. You can also write directly onto some bags with a black marker.

CHAPTER ONE
CHICKEN

Chicken Thighs
with Potatoes and Carrots

This simple recipe calls for carrots, potatoes, and chicken thighs simmered in spices and chicken broth. You'll love the delicious results of this straightforward recipe.

6 bone-in chicken thighs

1 cup chopped frozen onion

4 potatoes, chopped

2 cups sliced frozen carrots

½ cup chicken broth

SEASONINGS

1 teaspoon garlic powder

½ teaspoon dried thyme

1 teaspoon paprika

Salt and pepper, to taste

Dump all ingredients into the slow cooker. Cook on low for 6 hours.

> "One of the very nicest things about life is the way we must regularly stop whatever it is we are doing and devote our attention to eating."
> —Luciano Pavarotti

Spicy Chicken Avocado Soup

The avocado in this recipe helps tone down the spice from the chili flakes and salsa verde for a perfectly balanced and fresh-tasting soup. This is a great dish to enjoy in the summer when you want something light but flavorful. Add some shredded cheese, corn, and cilantro for a garnish and serve with tortilla chips.

6 cups chicken broth

2 boneless chicken breasts

2 (15-ounce) cans Great Northern beans, drained

2 cups salsa verde, medium or hot

2 avocados, sliced

SEASONINGS

1 teaspoon chili flakes

1 teaspoon cumin

Add the broth, chicken, beans, and salsa verde into the slow cooker and cook on low for 6 hours. Shred the chicken and add the avocado, chili flakes, and cumin just before serving.

Tip: Try serving with halves of cooked corn on the cob for visual interest.

Buffalo Blue Cheese Chicken Sliders

Tangy blue cheese dressing mixed with hot sauce gives these sliders a unique taste that's hard to beat—and the fresh crunchy cabbage adds just the right texture and color. Serve on a soft white bun and top with blue cheese crumbles.

4 boneless, skinless chicken thighs

1 cup water

2 cups hot sauce, divided

1 cup blue cheese dressing

2 cups red cabbage, sliced

8 to 10 mini rolls

Place the chicken, water, and 1 cup of hot sauce in the slow cooker. Cover and cook on low 6 hours. Shred the chicken with two forks, add the remaining hot sauce, and cook another 30 minutes. Serve on white buns and drizzle with the blue cheese dressing. Top with the red cabbage and garnish with blue cheese crumbles, if desired.

"Dear Lady, I beg you to cook as you please/But don't overlook the importance of cheese!"
—Ruth McCrea

Chicken Noodle Soup

With a rich, vegetable-infused broth that's simmered in the slow cooker for a full 8 hours, this tasty soup will soon become a household favorite. Whether you're nursing a cold or just keeping warm on a cold day this comforting soup will help make you feel better!

8 cups chicken broth

2 boneless, skinless chicken thighs

1 cup sliced frozen carrots

1 cup chopped frozen onion

1 (12-ounce) package of egg noodles

SEASONINGS

1 teaspoon garlic powder

1 teaspoon oregano

Salt and pepper, to taste

Add the broth, chicken, carrots, onion, garlic powder, oregano, salt, and pepper into the slow cooker. Cook on low for 7 hours, then add the egg noodles. Cook for another hour. Shred chicken before serving.

Shredded
Barbeque Chicken

This recipe was inspired by a friend based in Texas—so you know it's serious barbeque even if it is made in a handy slow cooker! This chicken barbeque is a lighter alternative to pork or beef and will make delicious sandwiches for a whole week. Top with shredded lettuce or cabbage.

3 cups barbeque sauce, divided

5 boneless, skinless chicken thighs

1 cup chopped frozen onion

¼ cup brown sugar

Reserving one half of the barbeque sauce, place all the ingredients in a slow cooker and cook on low for 6 hours. Remove and shred the chicken with two forks until you have bite-sized pieces. Return to the slow cooker and add the remaining barbeque sauce. Cook for another 15 to 20 minutes or until you're ready to serve.

"Here in Texas, barbeque is an obsession and the only cure for it is to eat some."
—Texas saying

Orange Chicken Drumsticks

Orange juice gives this tangy chicken dish some zing while the honey adds just the right amount of sweetness. Garnish with a handful of sesame seeds and some fresh cilantro and serve alongside a salad or rice.

8 chicken drumsticks, skin removed

⅓ cup honey

2 tablespoons orange juice

3 tablespoons soy sauce

1 tablespoon rice vinegar

SEASONINGS

2 tablespoons ground ginger

½ teaspoon red pepper flakes

Add the drumsticks to the slow cooker. Mix the rest of the ingredients in a bowl and pour over the chicken. Cook on low for 4 hours.

Herbed Roast Chicken

Slow cookers are perfect for making whole roast chicken that stays juicy and doesn't dry out. This one calls for a bit of your favorite white wine to give the chicken some flavor—an oaky Chardonnay or a dry Riesling both work well. With the leftovers you can make great sandwiches for the week.

1 (4-pound) whole chicken

½ cup chicken stock

¼ cup white wine

4 tablespoons butter

SEASONINGS

1 tablespoon thyme

1 tablespoon rosemary

1 tablespoon parsley

1 tablespoon chopped garlic

Salt and pepper, to taste

Add the butter, chicken, stock, and wine to the slow cooker. Sprinkle thyme, rosemary, parsley, garlic, salt, and pepper on top. Cook on low for 8 hours. Garnish with a slice of lemon and more herbs.

Italian Parmesan Chicken

This Italian Parmesan Chicken calls for Italian dressing to create a moist, tender chicken breast and melt-in-your mouth carrots and potatoes. It also contains all four food groups so you can rest assured you're serving up a well-balanced meal!

2 cups Italian salad dressing

4 boneless chicken breasts

½ cup Parmesan cheese, shredded

½ bag of mini carrots

Add a few tablespoons of salad dressing to the slow cooker and place two chicken breasts on top followed by more salad dressing and half the cheese. Add the remaining two chicken breasts and the remaining cheese followed by the carrots. Cover with salad dressing. Cook on low for 6 hours.

Dad's Famous Chicken Curry

This chicken, potato, and mushroom curry is a delicious recipe that comes from my father. He's been making this dish for decades and each time he tries something new—and so can you! It's a great basic recipe for those looking to experiment. Variations might include adding some chopped bell pepper, eggplant, carrots, or sugar snap peas. Enjoy!

3 boneless chicken breasts

1 cup chopped frozen onion

1 (8-ounce) package pre-sliced mushrooms

4 potatoes, cubed

1 (14-ounce) can of stewed tomatoes

1 cup water

SEASONINGS

2 tablespoons curry paste

2 teaspoons garlic

2 teaspoons ginger

2 teaspoons turmeric

Add all the ingredients to the pot and cook on low for 8 hours. Serve on its own or with rice.

Salsa Verde
Chicken

Salsa verde means "green sauce" in Spanish, but don't let the simple name fool you. Salsa verde packs a flavorful punch—it gets its color from cilantro and green chilies. Pour a jar of it over few chicken breasts in the slow cooker and in just a few hours you'll have a tangy, juicy chicken dinner the whole family will enjoy. And remember, salsa verde can vary depending on the brand you choose, so try experimenting with different kinds until you find one that hits your sweet spot—not too spicy, or just spicy enough!

2 bone-in chicken breasts, skin removed

1 (16-ounce) jar of salsa verde

Add the chicken breasts to the slow cooker and cover with the salsa verde. Cook on low for 6 to 8 hours. Serve with rice or a side salad.

"I am not a glutton. I am an explorer of food."

—Erma Bombeck

Sweet Potato and Kale Chicken Stew

This healthy, protein-packed stew is full of good-for-you foods. The kale, sweet potato, and chicken make for a light-tasting meal that will fill you up without feeling heavy.

2 boneless chicken breasts or thighs, cubed

2 large sweet potatoes, chopped

1 cup chopped frozen onion

1 (15-ounce) can stewed tomatoes

4 cups kale, chopped

SEASONINGS

½ teaspoon garlic powder

1 bay leaf

Salt and pepper, to taste

Add all the ingredients except the kale into the slow cooker. If mixture seems dry, add 1 cup water. Cook on low for 6 hours. Add the kale and cook another 20 minutes or until kale is tender.

"The body becomes what the foods are, as the spirit becomes what the thoughts are."
—Kemetic saying

Chicken and Cashew Medley

Crunchy cashews and tangy chicken are what's on the menu tonight. This recipe calls for a heaping cup of delicious cashews to be added to the slow cooker at the last minute. The crunchy texture works perfectly with the tender chicken. Garnish with a handful of sesame seeds and some green onion.

- 4 boneless, skinless chicken thighs
- 4 tablespoons cornstarch
- ½ cup soy sauce
- 4 tablespoons rice wine vinegar

SEASONINGS

- 1 teaspoon ginger powder
- 1 teaspoon garlic powder
- 1 teaspoon chili flakes
- Salt and pepper, to taste
- 1 cup cashews

Place chicken and cornstarch in a Ziploc bag and shake to coat the chicken. Add the chicken to the slow cooker along with the soy sauce, rice wine vinegar, and spices. Cook on low for 5 hours. Add cashews and cook for another hour. Garnish with chopped cilantro or spring onion and serve with rice.

Tip: If you want a sweeter taste, add two tablespoons of brown sugar to the mix.

Tuscan Chicken Alfredo

Creamy Alfredo sauce, tender chicken, and pasta with tomatoes and spinach make this Tuscan chicken Alfredo a treat for the whole family. Have fun choosing the Alfredo sauce—whether you love garlic or cheese there's a specialty sauce with a flavor just for you. Garnish with a bit of Parmesan cheese and serve with crusty garlic bread.

3 boneless chicken breasts

1 (15-ounce) jar Alfredo sauce

½ cup sun-dried tomatoes, chopped

1 (10-ounce) package frozen spinach

½ pound fettuccini pasta, cooked

SEASONINGS

1 teaspoon dried onion

1 teaspoon garlic powder

Salt and pepper

Add the chicken, Alfredo sauce, and spices to the pot. Cook on low for 4 to 6 hours. Add the tomatoes, spinach, and pasta, and cook for another 5 to 10 minutes or until new ingredients are warmed. Garnish with some Parmesan cheese and serve with garlic bread.

> "The trouble with eating Italian food is that five or six days later you're hungry again."
> —George Miller

Chicken Tikka Masala

Chicken Tikka Masala is a mild, creamy Indian dish that's all about the spices. This recipe calls for Garam Masala, which is a premade mixture of Indian spices like cloves, cinnamon, and nutmeg that you can find in most grocery stores. If you don't have any on hand you can probably make some using what's already in your spice collection! Serve with some basmati rice and garnish with chopped cilantro.

1 pound boneless, skinless chicken thighs, cubed

1 cup chopped frozen onion

¾ cup coconut milk

1 (28-ounce) can of stewed tomatoes

SEASONINGS

2 tablespoons Garam Masala (Indian spice mix available at most grocery stores)

2 teaspoons paprika

2 teaspoons salt

2 teaspoons garlic powder

1 teaspoon ground ginger

Place all ingredients in the slow cooker ensuring the spices are dissolved in the coconut milk and stewed tomato mixture. Cook on low for 8 hours. Serve over some white rice and garnish with some chopped cilantro.

Drunken Cornish Hens

A tender twosome of Cornish hens simmered in white wine and hearty broth. This is a perfect dish for a special occasion like Thanksgiving or Valentine's Day.

2 Cornish hens

1 stick butter

1 ½ cups chicken broth

1 bottle of white wine

12 baby carrots, sliced lengthwise

SEASONINGS

3 teaspoons rosemary

2 tablespoons garlic powder

Salt and pepper, to taste

Fresh parsley, optional

Rub the birds all over with butter and season with salt and pepper. Place the onion, rosemary, garlic powder, and any extra butter in the slow cooker. Place the birds on top and cover with the bottle of white wine and the chicken broth. Cook on low for 8 hours. Sprinkle with parsley, if using.

"I enjoy cooking with wine, sometimes I even put it in the food."
—Julia Child

Slow Cooker
Pot Pie

Cream of chicken soup, chicken, and vegetables all combine to make this thick and creamy pot pie! This works well served with a crusty piece of bread and topped with heaps of shredded cheddar cheese.

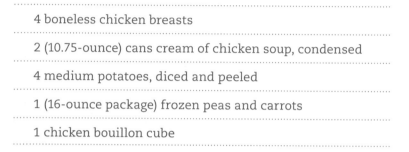

4 boneless chicken breasts

2 (10.75-ounce) cans cream of chicken soup, condensed

4 medium potatoes, diced and peeled

1 (16-ounce package) frozen peas and carrots

1 chicken bouillon cube

Combine all the ingredients in a slow cooker and cook on low for 6 hours. Shred chicken with two forks. Serve with some crusty bread and garnish with a handful of shredded cheese.

"There is nothing better on a cold wintry day than a properly made pot pie."
—Craig Claiborn

Chicken-Apple
Sausage with
Sweet Potatoes

This sweet twist on traditional potatoes is a perfect dish for autumn or winter. The chicken-apple sausage makes a great accompaniment to the sweet potatoes.

4 sweet potatoes, peeled and cubed

1 (12-ounce) package chicken-apple sausages, sliced

½ cup sliced frozen peppers

1 cup apple juice

⅔ cups brown sugar

SEASONINGS

1 teaspoon cinnamon

1 teaspoon thyme

Salt and pepper, to taste

Place all the ingredients in a slow cooker. Cook on low for 6 hours or until sweet potatoes are tender. Garnish with some cilantro or chopped pecans.

"When my mother had to get dinner for 8, she'd make enough for 16 and only serve half."
—Gracie Allen

CHAPTER TWO

PORK

Kale, Sausage, and White Bean Soup

This flavorful soup isn't just tasty—it's also good for you! With nutrient-rich kale and protein-packed white beans, this recipe is a perennial favorite in my family. If you want a vegetarian version, just use a vegetable broth and swap out the sausage for some fresh tofu or add an extra handful or two of kale.

4 cups chicken broth

3 mild Italian sausages, sliced

1 cup chopped frozen onion

1 (15-ounce) can Great Northern beans, drained

1½ cups kale, chopped

SEASONINGS

1 teaspoon garlic powder

Salt and pepper, to taste

Add broth, sausage, onion, beans, and spices to the slow cooker.
Cook on low for 6 hours. Add kale and let it cook for an additional hour or until cooked.

Simple Sausage Jambalaya

Jambalaya is a Creole dish from Louisiana that has both Spanish and French influences. Smoky Andouille sausage gives this dish a lot of flavor—but feel free to improvise! Shrimp is a great addition to any jambalaya, but this quick and easy version is a great starting point.

½ pound Andouille sausage, thinly sliced

1 (10.75-ounce) can French onion soup

1 (15-ounce) can diced tomatoes

1 (15-ounce) can black-eyed peas with bacon

2 cups cooked rice

SEASONINGS

1 tablespoon Creole mix

Salt and pepper, to taste

Add all the ingredients into the slow cooker. Cook on low for 6 to 8 hours.

"The discovery of a new dish does more for the happiness of mankind than the discovery of a star."
—Jean Anthelme Brillat-Savarin

Kielbasa and Carrot Medley

This is a quick recipe with just five ingredients that tastes absolutely heavenly!

1 pound kielbasa, sliced

1 cup brown sugar

1 cup ketchup

½ cup applesauce

1 cup baby carrots

Add all the ingredients to the slow cooker and stir to combine. Cook on low for 5 hours or until carrots are tender. Serve with rice if desired.

"Strange to see how a good dinner and feasting reconciles everybody."
—Samuel Pepys

Rosemary Herbed Pork Chops

There's something about rosemary that just works perfectly with pork. These juicy pork chops seasoned with rosemary are a fragrant, tasty delight. Serve with mashed potatoes or a side of rice.

4 thick-cut pork chops, bone in

1 (10.75-ounce) can cream of mushroom soup, condensed

1 (1-ounce) envelope dried onion soup mix

1 (4.5-ounce) can mushroom slices

1 cup chicken broth

SEASONINGS

1 teaspoon rosemary

1 teaspoon pepper

1 teaspoon garlic powder

Place the pork chops in the slow cooker and add remaining ingredients on top. Stir to ensure soup mix is dissolved. Cook on low for 6 hours. Remove rosemary sprigs before serving.

Pulled Pork

Everyone loves a tender, juicy, flavorful pulled pork sandwich. Whether it's the Fourth of July or Super Bowl Sunday, this pulled pork is sure to be a crowd pleaser. Serve on a fresh white bun for maximum enjoyment.

2 cups chopped frozen onion

1 (4–5 pound) boneless pork shoulder roast

1 (10.75-ounce) can chicken broth

1 cup barbeque sauce

SEASONINGS

1 tablespoon garlic powder

1 teaspoon salt

Place the onions in the slow cooker. Rub the roast with the garlic and salt and place on top of the onions. Cover with the broth. Cook for 8 hours on low or until the meat shreds easily with a fork.

"Too few people understand a really good sandwich."

—James Beard

Baby Back Ribs

If you've never made ribs in a slow cooker get ready for some fall-off-the-bone deliciousness! Just pop them in your slow cooker and 8 hours later they're ready to enjoy. I serve mine with some Parmesan-crusted corn on the cob.

2½ pounds baby back pork ribs

1 cup barbeque sauce

Cut the ribs into single servings—usually 3 to 4 ribs per serving is a good size. Place the ribs into a greased, aluminum foil–lined slow cooker. Cook on low for 8 hours. Remove and brush with the barbeque sauce.

Tip: After you've brushed the barbeque sauce onto the ribs try placing them under the broiler for about 5 minutes to really marry the flavors.

Potato Bacon Casserole

This casserole has a delicious smoky/salty flavor thanks to the bacon and is a great comfort food on a cold day. If you miss the characteristic crunchy top you get with baked casseroles, add a handful of crushed potato chips before serving.

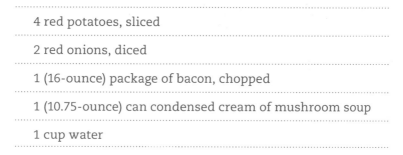

4 red potatoes, sliced

2 red onions, diced

1 (16-ounce) package of bacon, chopped

1 (10.75-ounce) can condensed cream of mushroom soup

1 cup water

Add all ingredients into the slow cooker and cook on low for 6 hours or until potatoes are firm but tender. Garnish with some spring onions, grated cheddar cheese, or potato chips for some crunch.

"There is no love sincerer than the love of food."

—George Bernard Shaw

Bacon Baked Beans

The bacon gives this dish a savory twist. Serve this with a piece of crusty bread.

2 (15-ounce) cans Great Northern beans, drained

½ cup barbeque sauce

½ cup ketchup

1 cup frozen chopped onions

4 slices bacon, diced

Add all ingredients to the slow cooker and stir until mixed. Cook on low for 6 hours.

Tip: If you want a vegetarian option, try swapping the bacon for a chopped green bell pepper or onion.

Breakfast-For-Dinner Casserole

Prepare this tasty breakfast casserole the night before and enjoy it in the morning when you wake up—or enjoy this eggy dish for dinner. This casserole can be made healthier by swapping the bacon for some broccoli or bell pepper.

1 (32-ounce) bag frozen hash browns

6 pieces ham, diced

1 cup chopped frozen onion

1 cup shredded cheddar cheese

10 eggs

SEASONINGS

Salt and pepper, to taste

Add half the hash browns to a greased, aluminum foil–lined slow cooker. Add half the ham, onion, and cheese. Top with the remaining hash browns, ham, onion, and cheese. Beat the eggs and pour them over the mixture. Season with salt and pepper to taste. If you need more liquid to cover the ingredients try adding a half cup of whole milk. Cook on low for 8 hours.

CHAPTER THREE
BEEF

Broccoli Beef

Broccoli Beef is a much-loved Chinese-American classic. While real Chinese broccoli, gai lan, is actually a different, leafier vegetable than American broccoli, the satisfying crunchy texture is the same. Serve over white rice for a healthy meal.

1 pound boneless chuck, sliced

1½ cups broccoli florets

¼ cup teriyaki sauce

½ tablespoon sesame oil

1 cup beef broth

SEASONINGS

2 tablespoons garlic powder

Salt and pepper, to taste

Add all the ingredients together in the slow cooker and cook on high for 3 hours. Serve with white rice.

Beef Brisket

This classic beef brisket will be sure to satisfy any meat lover. The onion and garlic flavors meld perfectly in this dish to create a full, rich, meaty taste that your friends and family won't be able to resist. Pile the brisket on some white buns for delicious sandwiches or eat it alone with some collard greens or mac and cheese.

2½ cups beef broth

1 tablespoon olive oil

2 pounds beef brisket

1 cup chopped frozen onion

1 tablespoon minced garlic

Add the broth and olive oil followed by the brisket. Add the onion and garlic to the top of the brisket. Cook on low for 6 hours or until the meat is very tender and the onions are soft. Don't forget the *au jus*!

Cowboy Beef Tacos

Ground beef and taco seasoning are the basis for this simple crowd-pleasing recipe. Once the taco filling is nice and hot, warm up some tortillas, fill with the seasoned meat, then top with shredded lettuce and cheese—and get ready to come back for seconds, or even thirds!

1 pound ground beef

1 (15-ounce) can diced tomatoes

1 (4-ounce) can green chiles

1 (12-ounce) package tortillas

2 cups shredded cheddar cheese

SEASONINGS

1 envelope taco seasoning mix

Place beef, tomatoes, green chiles, and seasoning into the slow cooker and cook on low for 6 hours. Serve with warmed corn or flour tortillas. Garnish with your favorite taco toppings like tomatoes, shredded lettuce, and cheddar cheese.

"If more of us valued food and cheer and song above hoarded gold, it would be a merrier world."
—J. R. R. Tolkien

Corned Beef and Cabbage

Whether you're celebrating your Irish heritage or celebrating St. Patrick's Day (or both) this is a quick and easy way to enjoy a taste of the Emerald Isle. If you're feeling adventurous, add half a can of beer to bring out the flavors of the brisket.

3 pounds corned beef brisket

10 baby red potatoes, chopped

1 cup chopped frozen onion

4 cups water

½ head cabbage, chopped

Add the brisket, potatoes, onion, and water (and beer, if using) into the slow cooker and cook on high for 7 hours. Add the chopped cabbage and cook for another hour or until cabbage is tender. Serve with a pint of Guinness for maximum enjoyment!

"A cabin with plenty of food is better than a hungry castle."

—Irish proverb

Classic Chili

Ground beef marinated with delicious chili spices—this recipe is a classic chili for the whole family. So if you've never tried chili in the slow cooker, start with this basic recipe and get creative from there! This dish can be adapted for any taste, so feel free to add some heat with jalapeños or extra chili powder as needed.

1 pound lean ground beef

1 (14-ounce) can tomato sauce

1 red bell pepper, chopped or 1 cup chopped frozen peppers

1 (15.5-ounce) can red kidney beans

1 cup chopped frozen onion

SEASONINGS

1 tablespoon ground cumin

1 tablespoon chili powder

Place all the ingredients in the slow cooker and cook on low for 8 hours.

Tip: If you like your chili spicy, add some chopped jalapeños.

"Savory seasonings stimulate the appetite."

—Latin Proverb

Cheesy Stuffed Peppers

These cheesy peppers make easy, self-contained meals that are sure to be a hit. Just lift them out of the pot and serve! If you want a healthier option, try ground turkey instead of ground beef or swap the rice for some cooked quinoa.

5 bell peppers

1 pound lean ground beef

1 (15-ounce) jar salsa

1 cup cooked rice

1 cup shredded cheddar cheese

SEASONINGS

Salt and pepper, to taste

Cut the tops from each pepper and scoop out the seeds. Combine the ground beef, salsa, rice, half the cheese, salt, and pepper. Stuff this mixture into each pepper. Fill the slow cooker with an inch of water and place the peppers in the pot. Cook on low for 6 hours. Top with the remaining cheddar cheese and serve.

Easy Beef Stroganoff

You'll want seconds of this classic stroganoff recipe: egg noodles covered in a thick mushroom gravy with tender beef and onion. Garnish with chopped cilantro.

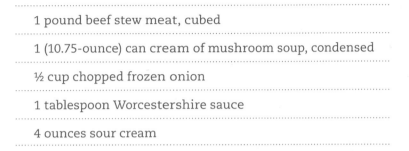

1 pound beef stew meat, cubed

1 (10.75-ounce) can cream of mushroom soup, condensed

½ cup chopped frozen onion

1 tablespoon Worcestershire sauce

4 ounces sour cream

In a slow cooker combine the meat, soup, onion, and Worcestershire sauce. Add a quarter cup of water to keep the beef moist. Cook on low for 8 hours. Stir in the sour cream right before serving. Serve atop a pile of egg noodles.

"Cooking well doesn't mean cooking fancy."

—Julia Child

Classic Family-Style Meat Loaf

A slow cooker recipe collection wouldn't be complete without one for good old-fashioned meat loaf. With this tangy loaf you'll have all the joy of classic meat loaf with none of the mess that comes from an oven-baked version.

- 2 pounds ground beef or mixture of beef and pork
- 1 (1-ounce) envelope dried onion soup mix
- 1 cup ketchup
- ¼ cup dry bread crumbs
- 1 egg

SEASONINGS

- 1 tablespoon Worcestershire Sauce
- 1 tablespoon yellow mustard

Combine the ground round, soup mix, half the ketchup, bread crumbs, and egg, and shape into a loaf. Line your slow cooker with lightly-greased aluminum foil along the bottom and sides, and place the loaf in the slow cooker. Top with a mixture of the Worcestershire Sauce, mustard, and remaining ketchup. Cook on low for 6 hours or until a meat thermometer registers 160 degrees. Brush with a bit of ketchup before serving for a nice glaze.

Tip: For an extra-moist meat loaf add ¼ cup of water to the slow cooker.

Steak and Mushrooms with Gravy

A thick meaty steak smothered in gravy and cooked to perfection . . . in a slow cooker? It's true! While it may seem like a form of sacrilege to prepare steaks in a slow cooker rather than on a grill, these delicious steaks will soon change your mind.

1 pound blade steak

1 (10.75-ounce) can cream of mushroom soup, condensed

1 envelope gravy mix

1 (8-ounce) package pre-sliced mushrooms

½ cup water

Add the ingredients to the slow cooker. Stir until onion powder and gravy mix are dissolved. Cook on low for 6 hours or until steaks are done to your liking.

Hearty
Shepherd's Pie

Baked Shepherd's pie is a real treat, but when you don't have time to watch the oven, this slow cooker version is a great alternative.

1 (10-ounce) package frozen mixed vegetables

1 pound lean ground beef

1 (12-ounce) jar gravy

2 cups instant mashed potatoes

SEASONINGS

1 teaspoon thyme

Salt and pepper, to taste

Add the frozen vegetables to the slow cooker and layer the meat overtop. Pour the gravy over the meat and add the thyme. Cook on low for 6 hours. Spoon the mashed potatoes on top and cook another 10 minutes. Serve in bowls and garnish with Parmesan cheese.

Italian Dip Sandwiches

This juicy beef-dip sandwich makes an incredibly satisfying meal. The juices from the meat tend to drip everywhere, soaking the bread and (if you're doing it right) generally making a bit of a mess. But man, does it taste good! Pile the meat onto a buttered, toasted roll, top with some mozzarella cheese, and serve alongside the juice from the pot for dipping. Grab a napkin, and enjoy!

3 pound chuck roast

2 (10.75-ounce) cans beef consommé

8 ounces (half a 16-ounce jar) pepperoncini peppers, drained

SEASONINGS

2 tablespoons oregano

1 tablespoon thyme

Place all the ingredients into the slow cooker. Cook on low for 6 hours. Shred the meat with two forks. Pile onto some toasted rolls and top with some mozzarella cheese. Serve with a side of the juice from the pot for dipping.

Family-Style
Pot Roast

This pot roast is one of the simplest, heartiest slow cooker meals out there. This is the perfect dinner for a cold day in winter when there's snow on the ground and you need something tasty to warm you up! Garnish with some chopped spring onion for a fresh crunch.

1 (2-pound) roast

2 cups sliced frozen carrots

2 cups potatoes, chopped

1 cup chopped frozen onion

2 cups beef broth

SEASONINGS

1 tablespoon parsley

Place the ingredients in the slow cooker and cook on high for about 6 hours.

"Vegetables are interesting but lack a sense of purpose when unaccompanied by a good cut of meat."
—Fran Lebowitz

BBQ Meatball Sandwiches

These barbeque-slathered meatball sandwiches make a great game-day meal. Pop them onto a roll, top with mozzarella, and get ready to come back for seconds. Remember the napkins!

1 (12-ounce) package frozen Italian meatballs

2¼ cups barbeque sauce

¼ cup brown sugar

½ cup shredded mozzarella cheese

Add the meatballs, sauce, and sugar, to the slow cooker and stir until meatballs are coated. Cook on high for 3 hours. Serve on a roll covered with mozzarella cheese.

TIP: Drizzle some extra barbeque sauce onto the sliders for an extra messy treat.

"Hunger is the best sauce in the world."

—Cervantes

Southwest
Meatball Stew

Meatballs served up with tomatoes, beans, and corn in a flavorful chicken broth will make this stew a family favorite. And while meatballs are pure Italian, the black beans and corn give this a Southwestern vibe you won't be able to resist!

1 (12-ounce) package frozen Italian meatballs

1 (15-ounce) can kidney beans

1 (14-ounce) can stewed tomatoes

1 (15-ounce) can of corn

1 (15-ounce) can of chicken broth

SEASONINGS

1 tablespoon oregano

Salt and pepper, to taste

Add all the ingredients into the slow cooker. Set on low and cook for 6 hours.

Quick and Easy
Lasagna

It may seem counterintuitive, but this lasagna recipe calls for ravioli! The reason is that using ready-made ravioli instead of layering the lasagna yourself cuts the prep time to virtually zero—without sacrificing flavor! Try this secret-shortcut recipe with lobster-stuffed ravioli for a decadent treat.

2 (9-ounce) packages frozen ravioli

1 (16-ounce) jar spaghetti sauce

3 cups shredded mozzarella cheese

Layer the ravioli, sauce, and cheese until the slow cooker is almost full. Cook on low for 3 hours.

"Life is a combination of magic and pasta."

—Federico Fellini

CHAPTER FOUR

FISH AND SEAFOOD

New England
Clam Chowder

Minced clams are the basis for this simple clam chowder recipe made with chunky potatoes, mushroom soup, and a healthy dose of black pepper. Garnish with shredded cheddar cheese or chopped bacon and serve with crackers.

1 (6-ounce) can minced clams

3 potatoes, chopped

1 cup chopped frozen onion

2 (12-ounce) cans evaporated milk

1 (10.75-ounce) can cream of mushroom soup, condensed

SEASONINGS

1 teaspoon oregano

1 teaspoon thyme

Salt and pepper, to taste

Drain the clams and reserve the juice. Refrigerate the clams. Place the clam juice and remaining ingredients in the slow cooker. Cook on low for 8 hours. Add the clams and cook another hour. Serve with crackers.

Hearty Shrimp Gumbo

This spicy gumbo recipe is highly adaptable according to your tastes. Instead of shrimp, try crawfish or chicken, or swap the shrimp and sausage for some okra and cooked rice for a vegetarian gumbo!

4 cups chicken broth

1 pound Andouille sausage, sliced

1 cup chopped frozen onion

½ cup flour

2 pounds cooked shrimp (frozen)

SEASONINGS

2 tablespoons Creole seasoning

1 tablespoon garlic powder

3 dried bay leaves

Combine everything except the shrimp in your slow cooker. Give everything a quick stir to ensure the seasoning and flour are dissolved in the broth. Cook on low for 6 hours. Add shrimp at end and cook until warmed through. Garnish with a few chopped spring onions.

Poached Salmon Fillets

Salmon is packed with essential vitamins like B12 and also contains heart-healthy omega 3 fatty acids. This simple recipe calls for the salmon to be poached and flavored with a bit of dill, some wine, and some broth. The best part? It only takes about 30 minutes! Garnish with fresh dill and serve with rice or new potatoes.

4 salmon fillets

1 cup chicken broth

¼ cup white wine

1 teaspoon dill

Salt and pepper

Place the ingredients into the slow cooker. Cook on low for 20 to 30 minutes or until salmon is cooked through. Garnish with some dill and a wedge of lemon.

"First we eat, then we do everything else."

—M. F. K. Fisher

CHAPTER FIVE

VEGETARIAN

Tortellini Soup

These tasty tortellini simmered in a hot chicken broth are always a hit with kids. Plus, with fresh green spinach and bright red tomatoes this soup looks as good as it tastes!

1 (19-ounce) package cheese tortellini, frozen

1 (16-ounce) frozen spinach

4 cups chicken broth

2 (15-ounce) cans diced tomatoes

1 block low-fat cream cheese

Add all the ingredients into the slow cooker. Cook on low for 3 hours.

"Worries go down better with soup."

—Jewish Proverb

Stuff-Your-Own
Baked Potatoes

This slow cooker recipe has just one ingredient. You guessed it—potatoes! What makes this recipe so awesome is that while the spuds are cooking all that's left to do is set up your baked potato-stuffing station! I recommend sour cream, chives, bacon bits, cheddar cheese . . . well, you get the idea!

4 Russet potatoes (or as many as you can fit in your slow cooker)

Prick each potato with a fork and wrap in aluminum foil. Place them in the pot and cook on low for 8 hours. Unwrap carefully and serve with toppings of your choosing.

"What I say is that, if a man really likes potatoes, he must be a pretty decent sort of fellow."
—A. A. Milne

Green Lentil Curry

Curry is one of those dishes that just tastes better when made with a slow cooker—all those spices need time to simmer! Coconut milk plus traditional Indian spices are what give these lentils their flavor. Garnish with some chopped tomatoes and fresh cilantro.

2 cups green lentils, rinsed

1 cup chopped frozen onion

3 ½ cups coconut milk

1 (5-ounce) can tomato paste

1 cup sliced frozen carrots

SEASONINGS

1 tablespoon garlic powder

1 teaspoon turmeric

1 teaspoon curry powder

1 teaspoon cumin

Dash of salt

Place all the ingredients in the slow cooker. Cook on low for 6 hours. Garnish with chopped tomatoes or cilantro.

Tip: If you check on the curry while it's cooking and feel like it needs more liquid, add a cup of hot water to the pot.

Country-Style
Macaroni and Cheese

It's true! You can make macaroni and cheese in your slow cooker—and it's delicious. While you can't leave this cooking all day (the pasta will overcook) this is a great one to make before running errands or on a weekend when you have more time at home. This rich, cheesy recipe will be sure to satisfy even the hungriest stomachs.

2 cups cooked elbow macaroni

2 large eggs, beaten

5 cups grated cheddar cheese, grated

2½ cups whole milk

¼ cup butter

SEASONINGS

1 teaspoon salt

Dash of pepper

Dash of paprika

Mix the cooked macaroni, eggs, 4 cups of cheddar cheese, milk, butter, and seasonings until blended and add to the slow cooker. Sprinkle the reserved cup of cheese over the top of the mixture. Cook on low for 3 hours. Stir before serving. Garnish with Parmesan cheese, or more cheddar, if desired.

Black Bean and Corn Enchiladas

This simple vegetarian recipe uses corn and black beans but you can easily add ground beef. Just fill your tortillas, wrap them tight, and let your slow cooker do the work!

1 (15-ounce) can black beans, drained and rinsed

1 (15-ounce) can corn, drained

2 cups shredded cheddar cheese, divided

12 corn or flour tortillas

1 (24-ounce) jar salsa

Mash the black beans with a fork or potato masher. Stir in the corn, salt, cumin, and 1 cup of cheese and mix well. Spoon the mixture evenly onto the tortillas, then roll them up. Add a few tablespoons of salsa to the slow cooker and place the tortillas on top, seam side down. Cover with the remaining salsa and cheese. Cook on low for 3 to 4 hours. Serve with rice or guacamole.

Two Corn Chowder

Creamed corn and kernelled corn double up to make this corn chowder twice as nice. A few diced green chilies give this recipe a bit of a kick. Serve with some crusty bread and top with a few pieces of avocado or some shredded cheddar cheese.

3 red potatoes, diced

2 (15-ounce) cans creamed corn

1 (15-ounce) can whole kernel corn, drained

1 (10.75-ounce) can chicken broth, condensed

1 (4-ounce) can diced green chilies

SEASONINGS

1 teaspoon dried parsley

Salt and pepper, to taste

Add all the ingredients into the slow cooker. Cook on low for 6 hours or until potatoes are tender. Garnish with shredded cheddar cheese or avocado.

"Chowder breathes reassurance. It steams consolation."
—Clementine Paddleford

Acknowledgments

Thanks to friends and family who contributed suggestions for slow cooker recipes: Tiffany Antone, Rachel Brookhart, Terry McCartney, Jacquie Ogilvie, Kyle Shaughnessy, Mara Shaughnessy, Nicky White, and Andrea Young.

Index

A

Alfredo, Tuscan Chicken, 41
Andouille sausage
    in Hearty Shrimp Gumbo, 106
    Simple Sausage Jambalaya, 54
Avocado Soup, Spicy Chicken, 18

B

Baby Back Ribs, 62
bacon
    Bacon Baked Beans with Broccoli, 66
    Potato Bacon Casserole, 65
Baked Potatoes, Stuff-Your-Own, 114
barbeque sauce
    in Baby Back Ribs, 62
    in Bacon Baked Beans with Broccoli, 66
    BBQ Meatball Sandwiches, 97
    Shredded Barbeque Chicken, 25
BBQ Meatball Sandwiches, 97
beans. See also kidney beans; Northern
    beans
    Black Bean and Corn Enchiladas, 121
beef. See also ground beef
    Beef Brisket, 74
    Broccoli Beef, 73
    Corned Beef and Cabbage, 78
    Easy Beef Stroganoff, 85
    Family-Style Pot Roast, 94
    Italian Dip Sandwiches, 93
    Steak and Mushrooms with Gravy, 89
Beef Brisket, 74
Black Bean and Corn Enchiladas, 121
black-eyed peas with bacon, in Simple Sau-
    sage Jambalaya, 54
blue cheese dressing, in Buffalo Blue Cheese
    Chicken Sliders, 21
Breakfast-For-Dinner Casserole, 69
broccoli
    Bacon Baked Beans with Broccoli, 66
    Broccoli Beef, 73
Buffalo Blue Cheese Chicken Sliders, 21

C

cabbage
    in Buffalo Blue Cheese Chicken Sliders, 21
    Corned Beef and Cabbage, 78
carrots
    in Chicken Noodle Soup, 22
    Chicken Thighs with Potatoes and Car-
      rots, 17
    in Family-Style Pot Roast, 94
    in Green Lentil Curry, 117
    in Italian Parmesan Chicken, 30
    Kielbasa and Carrot Medley, 57
Cashew and Chicken Medley, 38
cheddar cheese
    in Black Bean and Corn Enchiladas, 121
    in Breakfast-For-Dinner Casserole, 69
    in Cheesy Stuffed Peppers, 82
    Country-Style Macaroni and Cheese, 118
Cheesy Stuffed Peppers, 82
chicken
    Buffalo Blue Cheese Chicken Sliders, 21
    Chicken and Cashew Medley, 38
    Chicken-Apple Sausage with Sweet Potatoes,
      49
    Chicken Noodle Soup, 22
    Chicken Thighs with Potatoes and Car-
      rots, 17
    Chicken Tikka Masala, 42
    Dad's Famous Chicken Curry, 33
    Herbed Roast Chicken, 29
    Italian Parmesan Chicken, 30
    Orange Chicken Drumsticks, 26
    Salsa Verde Chicken, 34
    Shredded Barbeque Chicken, 25
    Slow Cooker Pot Pie, 46
    Spicy Chicken Avocado Soup, 18
    Sweet Potato and Kale Chicken Stew, 37
    Tuscan Chicken Alfredo, 41
Chicken and Cashew Medley, 38
Chicken-Apple Sausage with Sweet Potatoes,
    49
Chicken Noodle Soup, 22
Chicken Thighs with Potatoes and Carrots,
    17
Chicken Tikka Masala, 42
Chili, Classic, 81
Clam Chowder, New England, 105
Classic Chili, 81
Classic Family-Style Meat Loaf, 86
coconut milk
    in Chicken Tikka Masala, 42
    in Green Lentil Curry, 117
corn
    Black Bean and Corn Enchiladas, 121
    in Southwest Meatball Stew, 98
    Two Corn Chowder, 122
Corned Beef and Cabbage, 78
Cornish Hens, Drunken, 45
Country-Style Macaroni and Cheese, 118
Cowboy Beef Tacos, 77

cream of chicken soup, in Slow Cooker Pot Pie, 46

cream of mushroom soup
in Easy Beef Stroganoff, 85
in New England Clam Chowder, 105
in Potato Bacon Casserole, 65
in Rosemary Herbed Pork Chops, 58
Steak and Mushrooms with Gravy, 89

curries
Dad's Famous Chicken Curry, 33
Green Lentil Curry, 117

D

Dad's Famous Chicken Curry, 33

diced tomatoes
in Cowboy Beef Tacos, 77
in Simple Sausage Jambalaya, 54
in Tortellini Soup, 113

Drunken Cornish Hens, 45

E

Easy Beef Stroganoff, 85
egg noodles, in Chicken Noodle Soup, 22
eggs, in Breakfast-For-Dinner Casserole, 69
Enchiladas, Black Bean and Corn, 121

F

Family-Style Pot Roast, 94
fettuccini, in Tuscan Chicken Alfredo, 41

fish and seafood
Hearty Shrimp Gumbo, 106
New England Clam Chowder, 105
Poached Salmon Fillets, 109

French onion soup, in Simple Sausage Jambalaya, 54
frozen dinner preparation tips, 13

G

green chilies
in Cowboy Beef Tacos, 77
in Two Corn Chowder, 121

Green Lentil Curry, 117

ground beef
Cheesy Stuffed Peppers, 82
Classic Chili, 81
Classic Family-Style Meat Loaf, 86
Cowboy Beef Tacos, 77
Hearty Shepherd's Pie, 90

Gumbo, Hearty Shrimp, 106

H

ham, in Breakfast-For-Dinner Casserole, 69
hamburger. See ground beef

hash browns, frozen, in Breakfast-For-Dinner Casserole, 69
Hearty Shepherd's Pie, 90
Hearty Shrimp Gumbo, 106
Herbed Roast Chicken, 29

I

Italian Dip Sandwiches, 93
Italian Parmesan Chicken, 30
Italian sausages, in Kale, Sausage, and White Bean Soup, 53

J

Jambalaya, Simple Sausage, 54

K

kale
Kale, Sausage, and White Bean Soup, 53
Sweet Potato and Kale Chicken Stew, 37

kidney beans
in Classic Chili, 81
in Southwest Meatball Stew, 98

Kielbasa and Carrot Medley, 57

L

Lasagna, Quick and Easy, 101

M

Macaroni and Cheese, Country-Style, 118
mashed potatoes, instant, in Hearty Shepherd's Pie, 90

meatballs
BBQ Meatball Sandwiches, 97
Southwest Meatball Stew, 98

Meat Loaf, Classic Family-Style, 86

mozzarella cheese
in BBQ Meatball Sandwiches, 97
in Quick and Easy Lasagna, 101

mushrooms. See also cream of mushroom soup
in Dad's Famous Chicken Curry, 33
Steak and Mushrooms with Gravy, 89

N

New England Clam Chowder, 105

Northern beans
Bacon Baked Beans with Broccoli, 66
Kale, Sausage, and White Bean Soup, 53
in Spicy Chicken Avocado Soup, 18

O

onion soup mix, dried
in Classic Family-Style Meat Loaf, 86
in Rosemary Herbed Pork Chops, 58

Orange Chicken Drumsticks, 26

P
Parmesan Chicken, Italian, 30
pasta
   Country-Style Macaroni and Cheese, 118
   Tortellini Soup, 113
   Tuscan Chicken Alfredo, 41
pepperoncini peppers, in Italian Dip Sandwiches, 93
Poached Salmon Fillets, 109
pork
   Baby Back Ribs, 62
   Breakfast-For-Dinner Casserole, 69
   Kale, Sausage, and White Bean Soup, 53
   Kielbasa and Carrot Medley, 57
   Pulled Pork, 61
   Rosemary Herbed Pork Chops, 58
   Simple Sausage Jambalaya, 54
potatoes
   Chicken Thighs with Potatoes and Carrots, 17
   in Corned Beef and Cabbage, 78
   in Dad's Famous Chicken Curry, 33
   in Family-Style Pot Roast, 94
   in New England Clam Chowder, 105
   Potato Bacon Casserole, 65
   in Slow Cooker Pot Pie, 46
   Stuff-Your-Own Baked Potatoes, 114
Pot Pie, Slow Cooker, 46
Pot Roast, Family-Style, 94
Pulled Pork, 61

Q
Quick and Easy Lasagna, 101

R
rice
   in Cheesy Stuffed Peppers, 82
   in Simple Sausage Jambalaya, 54
Roast Chicken, Herbed, 29
Rosemary Herbed Pork Chops, 58

S
Salmon Fillets, Poached, 109
salsa
   in Black Bean and Corn Enchiladas, 121
   in Cheesy Stuffed Peppers, 82
salsa verde
   Salsa Verde Chicken, 34
   in Spicy Chicken Avocado Soup, 18
sandwiches
   BBQ Meatball Sandwiches, 97

Beef Brisket, 74
Buffalo Blue Cheese Chicken Sliders, 21
Italian Dip Sandwiches, 93
Pulled Pork, 61
Shredded Barbeque Chicken, 25
Shepherd's Pie, Hearty, 90
Shredded Barbeque Chicken, 25
Shrimp Gumbo, Hearty, 106
Simple Sausage Jambalaya, 54
Slow Cooker Pot Pie, 46
slow cookers
   choosing, 9–10
   tips for healthy cooking, 10
   tips for using, 12
soups
   Chicken Noodle Soup, 22
   Kale, Sausage, and White Bean Soup, 53
   New England Clam Chowder, 105
   Spicy Chicken Avocado Soup, 18
   Tortellini Soup, 113
   Two Corn Chowder, 122
Southwest Meatball Stew, 98
spaghetti sauce, in Quick and Easy Lasagna, 101
Spicy Chicken Avocado Soup, 18
spinach
   in Tortellini Soup, 113
   in Tuscan Chicken Alfredo, 41
Steak and Mushrooms with Gravy, 89
stewed tomatoes
   in Chicken Tikka Masala, 42
   in Dad's Famous Chicken Curry, 33
   in Southwest Meatball Stew, 98
   in Sweet Potato and Kale Chicken Stew, 37
Stroganoff, Easy Beef, 85
Stuff-Your-Own Baked Potatoes, 114
sweet potatoes
   Chicken-Apple Sausage with Sweet Potatoes, 49
   Sweet Potato and Kale Chicken Stew, 37

T
Tacos, Cowboy Beef, 77
teriyaki sauce, in Broccoli Beef, 73
Tikka Masala, Chicken, 42
tomatoes. *See also* diced tomatoes; stewed tomatoes
   sun-dried, in Tuscan Chicken Alfredo, 41
Tortellini Soup, 113
Tuscan Chicken Alfredo, 41
Two Corn Chowder, 122